Yes, There Will Be Singing

HAMRAAZ

cntxt

Published by Context, an imprint of Westland Books, a division of Nasadiya Technologies Private Limited, in 2024

No. 269/2B, First Floor, 'Irai Arul', Vimalraj Street, Nethaji Nagar, Alapakkam Main Road, Maduravoyal, Chennai 600095

Westland, the Westland logo, Context and the Context logo are the trademarks of Nasadiya Technologies Private Limited, or its affiliates.

Copyright © Hamraaz, 2024

Hamraaz asserts the moral right to be identified as the author of this work.

ISBN:

10 9 8 7 6 5 4 3 2 1

This is a work of fiction. Names, characters, organisations, places, events and incidents are either products of the author's imagination or used fictitiously.

All rights reserved

Typeset by Jojy Philip, New Delhi
Printed at

No part of this book may be reproduced, or stored in a retrieval system, or transmitted in any form or by any means, electronic, mechanical, photocopying, recording, or otherwise, without express written permission of the publisher.

Yes, There Will Be Singing

For my partner, comrade and lover,
and for all those who refuse to stop singing

In the dark times
Will there also be singing?

Yes, there will be singing.
About the dark times.

— Bertolt Brecht, *The Svenborg Poems*

Contents

IN THE BEGINNING
August–December 2019

In the Beginning	3
On the Day of the Verdict	4
Hard Fruit	5

ECLIPSE
December 2019–February 2020

Mandi House	9
20 December: Rising	11
Eclipse	13
There Are Other Names for These Things	14
Not a Poem or a Song	15
In Praise of Azaadi	16
The Anti-Corruption CM Speaks His Mind	17
A Seditious Song!	18
Speak	20
Striding Man	21
Tender Comrade	23
It Is Difficult to Remember What Comes Next	24
What They've Been Feeding Us	25
Beyond the Horizon	26
Someday, After the Fire	28

We Have Been Here Before	29
We Must Insist on Saying Unspeakable Things	30
The Importance of Silence (or What Is to Be Done, Friends)	32
Pakistan Zindabad?	34
One More Precious Thing Has Been Sold	35
Fever Dreams and Rumours	36
In the Early Days of the Delhi Fires	38
We Cannot Fail to Write Love Poems	40

LOCKDOWN LULLABY
March–May 2020

What's Playing Now	45
Now We Must Depend on Those Who Are Near	46
It's Simple When You Think About It	47
Waiting at the Station	48
Some of Us, Friends	49
Small Confession	50
How Many, How Long?	51
Delhi Lockdown, 8.45 p.m.	52
Weather Report	53
Lockdown Lullaby	54
Green	55
PM Cares	56

NEWS ON THE STREET
May–August 2020

Ninety-nine Days After the Delhi Pogrom, While America Burned	59
News on the Street	60
Three Haiku (#SafooraZargar)	61
I Want to Go Back, Let's Go Back	62
Late Last Night	63
Someday We'll Remember How We Came Through This Together	64
He Does Most of His Work in the Dark	65
Catching Up in Strange Times	66
What Matters	67
So Long	68
Varavara Rao Came to Delhi Last Night	69
Welcoming the Storm	70
First, We Will Dream It	71
Last Week, in Hauz Rani Forest	72
Only Together Can We Bring It	73
Pinjra Tod	74
With All Due Respect to the Court	75
आवारा है	76

LIFTED AND CARRIED
September–November 2020

Lifted and Carried	81
I Think of Umar Khalid	83

Breaking	84
I Fall Asleep Reading a Poem by Akhil Katyal	85
Let Us All Rest in the Company of Those Who Love Us	86
Worried Blues Pantoum	87
Perhaps It's Best	88

NIGHTFALL AT SINGHU BORDER
November 2020–February 2021

Three Haiku	91
Nightfall at Singhu Border	92
Simple Definitions	93
Love Jihad	95
This Number Does Not Exist	96
13 Ways of Looking at a Farmer	98
Unshakeable	100
Kiss	101
The Moon the MHA and Agent Orange	102
My Mother Calls With Her Worries	104
You'll Join Us, I Know, My Friend	105
Like That Cat, or Our Constitution	106
A Question for the Court	107
Ghazal for a Capital in Darkness	108
Postcard from 2019	109

BEHIND THE MASK
February–April 2021

Change	113
Ten Letters	114

Behind the Mask	115
Note to a Fellow Poet on Subtlety and Silence	116
A Simple Prayer	118
Stopping by Saidulajaib to Consider Horses and Torture	119
Three Postcards to Umar Khalid	120
Still Trying	122
Coronation	123
News of Sickness and Health	124
Questions I Don't Need to Ask	125
Abolish Our Local Police	126
Reel for Delhi in Springtime	127

LATE APRIL PRAYER FOR DELHI
April–June 2021

Failure in Gujarat	131
A Late April Prayer for Delhi	132
I Have Seen Astonishing Sights	133
In Front of the Chemist	135
For a Tender Comrade	136
Delhi Emergency, 10 p.m.	137
Divinations	138
News in Review	139
For My Mother, That Baby and Father Stan Swamy	140

HOW IS IT WE KEEP FORGETTING
August 2021–June 2022

Failed Ghazal	143
Song for You	144
Elegy for Lakhimpur Kheri	145
Facing the NIA	146
Dreams of Fear and Rejoicing	147
What They're Selling	148
A Memory, a Prayer and a Dream	149
Sheep	151
The Censor at Work in the Park	152
'If they Are So mighty, Let Them Snuff Out the Moon'	153
Delhi Weekend Curfew	154
I Fall Asleep Reading Uday Prakash as Russia Invades Ukraine	155
Closer, Closer	157
How Is It We Keep Forgetting?	158
A War Poem	159
No Escape	160
Ghazal Against Bulldozers	161
Father Stan Swamy Came to Delhi Last Week	162
Acknowledgements	163

IN THE BEGINNING

August—December 2019

In the Beginning

I kept hearing people say
the same words over and over

wherever I went—
sometimes in greeting

or farewell,
sometimes in prayer—

the neighbour downstairs,
the electrician in the market,

the man who cleans
the toilet in the park.

The more it happened,
the more anxious I felt.

When I mentioned it to the chemist,
he lowered his voice and said,

*Yes, it's no longer just
a greeting or a prayer,*

*it's become a celebration—
and a challenge.*

On the Day of the Verdict
—*9 November 2019*

My barber closes the door and says,
He has everything in his hands now:

the parliament, army and courts;
his wish is our command now.

Hard Fruit

This morning, when I told you
that I'd dreamt

the theocracy had been declared—
and the internet was down

and it was no longer safe
to say 'freedom'

in songs or slogans,
or even on the phone—

you just nodded
and said you'd woken,

sweating and shaking,
after dreaming of breaking

all your front teeth on a hard,
red apple from Kashmir.

ECLIPSE

December 2019—February 2020

Mandi House
—*19 December 2019*

Though we had seen what
they did to the students,

something changed
that day in Delhi;

the police filled bus after bus
with people like us

who had come simply
to stand for our own rights

and for those of our neighbours.
Dropped on the edge of town,

hundreds returned to be taken again.
It is worse than we thought,

but I am fine now—
many have it much harder

is what you told the children.
Later you showed me

the boot-sized, black bruises
on both of your legs

and confessed you had cried
as you bathed.

20 December: Rising
—*for Chandra Shekhar Azad*

When they finally write the history
of how we finally won this fight,

they'll say the tide first turned
at Jama Masjid

when Chandra Shekhar Azad
held up the Constitution,

and a photo of Dr Ambedkar,
before leading the charge that freed

first Daryaganj, then Delhi
from the idea that we could be

so easily cowed and beaten.
That evening we all somehow knew

that somewhere in Lutyens' Delhi
the Home Minister was pacing

and pounding his fists on a wall—
and though the Chief

later turned himself in,
by then we all understood

that neither police nor army—
nor the devil himself

can turn back the sea
when it rises.

Eclipse
—26 December 2019

I dreamed a group of us
were kidnapped by a pair
of sociopaths—

they explained they were
conducting an experiment:
they would blind half of us

in one eye and half of us in both
to see how this would affect
our ability to love.

When I told you, you said:
*That's just a dream about
the leaders of our country.*

Later, the owner of a tea shack
handed us an X-ray of a broken foot
and gestured at the half-eaten sun.

There Are Other Names for These Things

Before the darkness
you used to laugh

when your Communist
friends warned you,

*Never forget the Golden Rule:
he who has the gold makes the rules!*

In UP, newspapers report
that police raided a madrasa

and arrested 100 young students
and a 66-year-old cleric

who they stripped naked
in the cold and tortured all night.

After their release,
some of the students said

they'd been beaten and forced
to chant *Jai Shree Ram*

while others came out crying,
bleeding from their rectums.

No one expects an investigation.

Not a Poem or a Song
—*for Shaheen Bagh*

Yesterday, you asked me to write a poem
or a song about the women of Shaheen Bagh,
and I laughed and said,
> that's not possible—
> the women of Shaheen Bagh
> *are* a poem *and* a song—

but last night as I drifted
off to sleep in my warm bed,
it came to me that I'd been wrong—
> the women of Shaheen Bagh
> are not a poem or a song,

they are *women* who have been sitting
for weeks, night and day, on a *road*—
> in spite of cold wind and hard pavement,
> in spite of the threat of lathis,
> tear gas and jail—

they've been sitting because they won't stand
> to see students beaten by police,
> to see unjust laws divide the land—
> because they are stubborn and right and strong—

and that, my friend, is more powerful and beautiful
than any poem or song.

In Praise of Azaadi
—*after Bertolt Brecht*

It's simple,
anyone can grasp it.
It requires no force
or violence.
The exploiters tell us
to sell, borrow and buy it;
pandits and priests
disguise it with dogma;
tyrants call it 'sedition'.
It is against buying, selling,
debt and dogma—
and 'sedition' sheds
all meaning in its presence.
The rulers call it worthless,
but we know:
it is *priceless*.
They have never
given it away freely—
we've had to seize it,
again and again.

It is the simplest thing,
so hard to hold on to.

The Anti-Corruption CM Speaks His Mind

Meanwhile in the capital, the CM speaks
at a town hall about unemployment,
the price of onions, and the danger
of Hindu spies from Pakistan.

He does not mention torture,
custodial rape and preventive detention
of citizens and politicians:
the gravest forms of modern corruption.

The next evening, at a Golf
Links wedding reception,
guests sipping wine
and Kashmiri kahwa
murmur and sigh as he
and his entourage sweep in
to greet the happy couple.

A Seditious Song!

I'm dreaming seditious dreams,
I'm singing a seditious song!
I'm loving my neighbours,
don't care where they're from—
let's abolish all checkpoints
    and borders…
as we sing a seditious song!

I'm dreaming seditious dreams,
I'm singing a seditious song!
I'm praying for freedom
from fear and from want—
let's plant crops, not walls,
    on our borders…
as we sing a seditious song!

I'm dreaming seditious dreams,
I'm singing a seditious song!
I'm reading Ambedkar,
he makes perfect sense—
let's annihilate things that
    divide us…
as we sing a seditious song!

I'm dreaming seditious dreams,
I'm singing a seditious song!
Some days let's be boys,

some days let's be girls—
let's fall in love when
    we want to…
as we sing a seditious song!

I'm dreaming seditious dreams,
I'm singing a seditious song!
Let's open libraries,
we'll read what we want—
we'll argue, and think
    together…
as we sing a seditious song!

I'm dreaming seditious dreams,
I'm singing a seditious song!
It's natural to cry,
to feel anxious and scared—
let's heal each other
    and struggle…
as we sing a seditious song!

Speak

> *'A girl, as part of the play's dialogue, spoke
> of beating anyone who would ever dare ask her
> for her documents with a chappal'.*
>
> – *The Wire*

The Emperor has no clothes:
every child knows this story—
our failure to say what we see;
dictators study this lesson.

Every child knows *this* story:
the bully who's secretly weak;
our rulers have studied this lesson—
why else charge a school with sedition?

A bully who's secretly weak,
or wolves or demons disguised;
why else charge a school with sedition?
What do they fear? A chappal?

Wolves or demons disguised,
our rulers depend on our silence;
What do they fear? A chappal—
or unafraid people who speak?

Our rulers depend on our silence;
our failure to say what we see—
But unafraid people will speak:
Where are the Emperor's clothes?

Striding Man
—*for Shadab Najar*

In the video, it all moves so fast,
but when the frame freezes,
some things become clear.

We see a boy or young man,
mouth wide, as if he
is smiling as he shouts—

in his right hand, a pistol;
it is pointed towards
the sky. Behind him,

a line of police look on,
one is leaning on his lathi;
to one side, a man aims a camera.

And now look at the man
with the long, wavy hair, striding
towards the man with the gun—

his arms are down,
his body open, as if to say,
I am not afraid of you,

*and you have nothing
to fear from me,*
as if to say,

*Hold on—
come, let's sit and talk.*
There is one more thing

every parent will see
when they study this photo
of the striding man:

someone, somewhere
raised this one right,
this one is one to be proud of.

Tender Comrade

In your dream, thin corpses
hang in a cold, dark room.

Strong men come and silently
slit them open;

they are harvesting handfuls
of organs—or pearls.

As you tell me this,
news of another Jamia shooting

and more election rally hatred
stream across screens all over Delhi.

What have I to offer,
tender comrade, friend?

Night has fallen,
the horizon is near,

we're all fighting
and longing for light.

It Is Difficult to Remember What Comes Next

It is difficult to remember when it was or could be, but the August sun was low, the air was clear and damp, and the roads were still, except for the rattle and ring of cycles and bells. We were walking through narrow lanes, offering to sing songs about the songs we'd all sung during the darkness. A few doors declined to open, and from time to time insults fell on us from behind shuttered windows: *infiltrator, anti-national, traitor*—and other hard words which no longer possessed any power or meaning. But on most corners, small crowds greeted us with shouts and hugs and many joined in when we sang. In the late afternoon, as we crossed a muddy field newly planted with tomato and pepper seedlings, a boy ran up from behind us and demanded to know if we remembered the song we'd been singing on Rajpath when the police threw down their lathis and guns and melted into the rising sea we'd all become. We solemnly nodded, then one of us sputtered, and we all started laughing and shouting and singing together. Later, we agreed that the song still tasted cool and sweet every time we sang it, like water drawn from a hand pump, like freedom.

What They've Been Feeding Us

This time, my barber does not lower
his voice as he announces:
They fed us hatred for weeks,

and a few do like the taste of that,
but most of us know it won't fill your belly—
the broom has swept Delhi again!

Later, you tell me about the persistent
pain in your stomach: *it's been a week,*
and I know it's just food poisoning,

but it feels different this time—
like I have a gut full of grief,
or dread.

Beyond the Horizon

In UP last year,
93,000 people applied
for 62 government jobs—

jobs that required
a Class 5 education
and bicycle riding skills;

of the applicants, 3,700
held PhDs, and 20,000
held postgraduate degrees.

You read these as signs:
harbingers of a rapidly
approaching turn

or fall—
Western environmentalists
call it a climate crisis

and offer a Green New Deal;
new communists call it
a secular crisis of capitalism

and say it is hopeless to try
to see beyond the horizon
of a system that conditions

even the way we make love.
We're all looking for a way
through: you, me,

the chief minister of UP,
and the crores who may
or may not have documents,

but who nonetheless haul
our trash, sweep our roads
and build our tall towers each day.

Some choose suicide or struggle,
some put their faith in fascism;
and some keep their heads

down and patiently wait
for some kind of a new
day to dawn.

Someday, After the Fire

The Delhi smoke is thick
    tonight, my love—

but here on this wide road,
    the wind is cool.

*Remember how it used
    to taste,* you say—

*like burning plastic, fear,
    and diesel fuel.*

This year, there is a new
    scent in the air,

like flowers blooming
    after a great fire.

I'm searching for a way
    back home again—

*Perhaps we'll build a better
    home,* you say.

We Have Been Here Before

I dreamt that, nearing his end,
my father wrote the story of his life
in the language of his grandmother.

I don't understand the words,
he told me, but I think you
will find it useful someday—

it has something to do
with the way we lived
in the dark times that came

before these dark times.
It is not easy to remember,
he told me. It has something

to do with scattered light,
and how I love you.

We Must Insist on Saying Unspeakable Things

When right-wing thugs
attack members of a religious
minority in broad daylight
in a nation's capital
while the police look on
or join in the attacks,
that is not a 'riot',
that is a *pogrom*.

And when armed men in uniform
force their way into homes,
break furniture and take
jewellery and cash,
that is not 'quelling a riot',
that is *loot* and *pillage*.

And when students of a madrasa
in UP, or any other place,
emerge from jail with bruises
and rectal bleeding,
that is not 'detention',
that is *torture* and *rape*.

And when officers of the law
take young men accused

of a crime to an empty field
(on a hillside or under a flyover),
and then turn them loose
and shoot them dead as they run,
that is not an 'encounter',
that is *murder*.

And when any government
anywhere in the world,
at any time in history,
accepts, justifies or orders
these and other crimes,
that is not a 'democracy',
that is *tyranny*.

And when any of us agree
to use words that mask
the truth of these
unspeakable things,
we are not using
 'measured language',
we are *telling lies*.

The Importance of Silence
(or What Is to Be Done, Friends)

Maybe you remember a class 5 teacher
who beat students, sometimes even
leaving bruises, and how he would tell
all the parents at Parent-Teacher Meetings
how much it hurt him to have to discipline
unruly children, and how the parents—
even, perhaps, *your* parents—
would nod sombrely, though they knew
he hit too hard.

Or maybe it was the professor who would
call quiet first-year students to his office
for extra help, *because he was so concerned
about their progress,* and everyone
in the class could see how uncomfortable
those students were, but no one said anything,
because, really, what was there to say,
except that he was so *concerned?*

Or maybe it was the husband of a neighbour
in your colony, who would tell everyone
how worried he was about his wife—
*she's seeing a doctor, you know,
sometimes she can't control her feelings—*
and everyone would nod, but also secretly
wonder: *does she scream because he beats her?*

Or maybe it was the prime minister
of a large country, who invited the president
of a more powerful country to visit
on the day that mobs of organised terrorists
were planning to burn homes, businesses
and places of worship, knowing the police
would stand by or join in, and maybe
that prime minister knew his guest
would not condemn this terror,
thus showing all of us that the world
was powerless to stop it, and maybe
he also knew that all over the capital
and country, people and leaders
and even respectable newspapers
would choose to use words like 'violent
demonstrations' and 'clashes' to describe
what they understood was probably
a *state-sponsored pogrom,*
and which might be the first step
towards something even graver.

If we think long and hard about this,
we may come to understand something
that every successful abuser, bully
and tyrant already knows—
the importance and power of *silence*—
and if we think even harder about the bravery,
solidarity and love that has sprouted in this city
and this country, in spite of the winter winds,
then we will know what we need to do now.
We will know what is to be done.

Pakistan Zindabad?

Why not? It's always better
when our neighbours prosper.

Also, Bangladesh zindabad,
and Myanmar, Bhutan, Sri Lanka…

In fact, why not just say,
saara jahaan zindabad?

What are we afraid of?
Let's say it together:

*Long live all the people
and creatures in this terrible,*

wonderful world we share.

One More Precious Thing Has Been Sold

Just three weeks ago, on the way
to the polling station

we saw a single, half-eaten
myna lying on the road.

Neither of us mentioned it;
the air was already

so heavy that day.
I no longer trust omens

and portents:
just last week, I dreamt

the HM was in jail,
but last night, I'm sure

I heard him whispering
in the CM's ear.

Fever Dreams and Rumours

Did you ever see Mani Ratnam's
film, *Bombay?*

In the midst of the terror,
an old man or woman—

it's difficult to remember now—
raised her hand and said:

Stop! Enough is enough!
And then all through the city,

brave men and women
stepped forward to say,

Ruk jao! Bas!
It was as if a great fever

had broken, and suddenly
they could see clearly again.

There was probably music playing,
and we all knew the director's

hand was there somewhere,
not so much saying,

'this is how it happened',
but 'this is how it *should*

have happened'.
Yesterday, we all heard

the rumours; at protest sites,
in markets, via Whatsapp

and Signal, they spread.
And late in the night,

as we lay awake,
trembling and praying—

Please, do not forget or forsake
us or our brothers and sisters—

none of us had any idea
if the fever had returned,

or who was directing this film.

In the Early Days of the Delhi Fires

We lay awake, trembling.
We no longer understood the rules,
      or where we were going.

We stopped posting selfies;
we flirted with memes
and sarcastic stories.

One by one, we got VPNs.
We shifted to Signal for politics,
gossip and love.

We could not put down
our phones; we could not bear
      to look at our phones.

We knew we had it better
than many. We knew it would
      get worse.

We fell in love at rallies,
argued on marches and tried
to forget what was coming.

Some of us were detained
and beaten. We knew many
had it worse.

We joked about the new virus—
we hugged each other and laughed
when we coughed.

Some of us called our parents,
some of us started smoking,
some of us secretly prayed.

We sang of heroes, cursed fascists,
shouted brave slogans, and worried.
      We were so tired.

Some days we thought we'd gone mad.
We remembered Kashmir;
      some of us drank too much.

Some nights, we gazed at the moon
from Jasola Vihar or Jamia.
      Some mornings, we woke up crying.

We Cannot Fail to Write Love Poems
—*after Miguel James*

If I write a poem against the CAA and the NRC,
that poem will be a love poem.
And if I write a poem about Chandra Shekhar Azad
leading a march in Daryaganj in support
of the Constitution and in violation of Section 144,
or a poem about hundreds of women sitting
day and night on the hard pavement of a main road
during the coldest months of the year,
or a poem that says what everyone knows—
that the police does not serve the people or our laws,
but only the Home Minister and his boss—
those, too, will be love poems.
If I write a poem against the very idea
of exploitation, property or borders,
or a poem about a ragged line of teenage boys,
trembling as they face a wall of police dressed
in riot gear and wielding lathis and guns,
and if one of those boys turns and runs,
while his friend reaches down and picks up
an egg-sized stone and weighs it in his hand
as he lets fly a word that means 'freedom'
but may later be translated as 'sedition'
in the court records if he is lucky enough
to live to appear in a court—

those, too, will be love poems.
All the poems that I and you and we
write and sing as we try to hold and show
the courage of people sitting
and standing and fighting
to be treated as human—
all of these may or may not fail
as poems, but not one of them
will fail to be a love poem.

LOCKDOWN LULLABY

March—May 2020

What's Playing Now

It's like that moment in the film
when the main characters

are looking out the window—
they can hear the thunder

and the rain, but the wind is still
just rustling the branches

and bushes in their small,
close-knit community

and it would look so peaceful,
except for the soundtrack

and the fact that you know
that they know

there is a mighty storm on the way,
and the only question

is whether it will be their home
or one of their neighbour's,

that will be left standing
after it passes.

Now We Must Depend on Those Who Are Near

Last night we argued on the phone—
like most of our quarrels

it was about something small,
and I think we both knew

it was really just a way to avoid
saying what is too difficult

to say right now:
you are so far away

and if you need me,
I have no way to reach you.

It's Simple When You Think About It

Why destroy art
at Shaheen Bagh

while locking
the country down?

Rulers who stand
for oppression,

fear pandemics—
but also expression.

Waiting at the Station

The night before the lockdown,
my sister called to say

our cousin had told her:
Go see your father soon,

he is not keeping well at all.
We both knew I could not go,

and that night I dreamed
I was standing alone

in a silent railway station,
waiting for something or someone.

And all week, I've been trying
to remember what I was waiting for:

was it my sister, my father,
or a train to take me home?

Some of Us, Friends

This city wakes daily
   to birdsong and worry—
we all miss our family
   or friends, or the sky;

we wonder how long
   our paychecks will last,
we fret about those who
   are sick, old or frail.

Some ask how long
   the aata will last,
will the police harass us
   if we go look for dal?

And some of us, friends,
   have no place to return to,
and some of us, friends,
   don't know how to get home—

and some of us, friends,
   are already hungry,
some of us, friends,
   are afraid and alone.

Distant or near,
   all of us matter,
we must not forget
   we depend on each other.

Small Confession

I just finished the story by Perumal Murugan
where a chair comes between a loving couple;
it's not controversial—

there's no inter-caste marriage or infidelity,
nothing to offend anyone's sensibilities
or to provoke the police, a court,

or a right-wing mob to ban or burn any books,
or threaten a mild-mannered author
with damnation or bodily harm—

there's just a man, a woman,
and a chair that slowly drives them apart.
Of course, the chair is a metaphor

for patriarchy and the many problems
that inevitably come with modernity—
like the wailing toilet in another

Murugan story, or this phone I use
to talk with the people I love,
and also to avoid them.

How Many, How Long?

How many summers have come
since Harappa and Mohenjo-daro
faded or fell?

We've all heard the story:
a river runs dry or changes course,
a new pestilence rides into town,

crops wither in baking fields.
Each time it happens must
seem like the first time—

hungry families camp outside
city gates or scatter like tumbleweed
towards faraway forests or hills

while rulers pace and wonder
how long their guard will hold.

Delhi Lockdown, 8.45 p.m.

Yes, hunger is stalking the land,
you've seen it up close, and I hear you.

And they are using the UAPA
to crush those who dare to speak out.

Last night, you lay awake turning,
I dreamt of thick smoke and my father—

but the moon is half full and waxing,
and the wind is gentle and clear;

let's grab our masks and a bag—
we'll walk towards a Mother Dairy;

I'll buy you a cold tadka chach,
you can buy me a cool, sweet lassi.

Weather Report

Yesterday's tomatoes pucker
on the kitchen counter,

and uneaten pulao turns
under a midnight fan.

Meanwhile in Surat,
police fire tear gas

at workers demanding
the right to go home—

beware my friends,
the season is changing

and there's more than one
sickness loose in the land.

Lockdown Lullaby

Let the ceiling fan spin you tonight,
>my friends,

>>you don't need to be anywhere.

Go lie on a cool, hard floor,
>my friends,

>>feel gravity hold you down.

Together, we've come through dark days,
>my friends,

>>there are darker days coming soon.

We're here for such a short while,
>my friends,

>>>the moon is flowering tonight.

Green

I dreamed I was writing in green,
my father was dressed in green robes—

the dogs in the park were frisking,
you were spinning beneath a tall tree.

I saw the capital emptied
of those who hungered for home—

two pigeons took flight from a lamp post
and swept down the lane in the back.

I heard they'd opened the jails
and freed all the wrongly accused,

I was writing this poem in green,
my father came close and he touched me.

PM Cares

I'm searching for scales to weigh what's fair:
families are hungry, miles from home;
don't worry, they say, our PM, he cares.

Millions are living on water and prayers,
while others are forced to work to the bone;
I'm still looking for scales to weigh what's fair.

It plays on the street, in the radio's blare,
listen, it's there, in the nightly news drone:
trust him, and give; our PM, he cares.

We need rations and love and protective gear,
we *must* care for *all* who are sick and alone;
we *have* to find scales to weigh what is fair.

We could file an RTI, if we dared:
'What matters more, food or free loans?'
Let's audit the PM: how *much* does he care?

We don't need police spreading hatred and fear,
we don't need new vistas, statues or thrones;
we'll fashion new scales, we'll weigh what is fair—
we'll learn from each other the meaning of *care*.

NEWS ON THE STREET

May–August 2020

Ninety-nine Days After the Delhi Pogrom, While America Burned

I dreamt they came to our door
and took you away at dawn.

I tried, but I could not stop them;
they were silent, and rough,

when you struggled.
Tonight, friends, let us all dream:

doors open and cages broken,
cool breezes and ceiling fans—

we'll argue and sing
and share what we have

*(we don't need the police,
we don't need the police!)*

News on the Street

Earlier in the week, the UP Police
charged a man with sedition

for calling CM Yogi a *dog* on FB,
and late last night,

the South Asian Canine Confederation
held emergency meetings

all over North India to debate
the difference between defamation

and free speech; you must have
heard them howling.

Three Haiku (#SafooraZargar)

Delhi Police blames
victims and those who preach peace;
they say *rain* is 'flame'.

Delhi judge accepts
unsaid words are sparks that blow;
court rules for the fire.

Delhi people know
rain is rain and fire is fire;
we're a rising sea.

I Want to Go Back, Let's Go Back

Let's float away on that rain cloud,
we could ride it over state lines,

we could ride it up north to the hills,
we could take off our masks and breathe deep.

Let's find us a cool, empty valley,
in a time before all this began,

we'll learn to dig roots from the ground,
we'll learn to dry fruit and to dance.

We'll study the way hard stone fractures,
we'll figure out fire and sing,

we'll forget about tear gas and prisons,
we'll live without curfews and kings.

Late Last Night

We slept on my grandmother's porch,
how we got there, who can say?

Dogs approached, snarling and circling;
I cried out, and you held me close.

Later, came sounds from the road,
a grinding of gravel and boots;

he came from the MHA;
he stunk of whisky and malice.

He said he'd be back in the morning,
whether or not I was pregnant—

as he left, the wind changed direction
and brought back the scent of still water.

Someday We'll Remember How We Came Through This Together

Behind us, a rusty wire fence; under our feet:
dry grass and dust. We were thirsty. Above us
loomed an enormous, leafless tree; it looked as if
it might touch the shivered June moon. Samir
gestured, or maybe it was Salima, and we all
leaned back and peered into the darkness. We
somehow understood that a piece of the tree, or
the moon, had broken off and was hurtling
towards us—but we had no idea where it might
land, so we just trembled and waited for thunder
and shake—or the end. Later, we tried to count
how many of us were missing. A woman ran
towards us, screaming. She was carrying a small
child in her arms. *His hand,* she sobbed.
It took only his hand.

He Does Most of His Work in the Dark

Every so often, I catch a glimpse
of the lizard that lives in my room;

he does most of his work in the dark.
I know it's a foolish comparison,

but his eyes evoke a home minister
who appears on the evening news.

Meanwhile, Safoora Zargar
has still not been granted bail,

and though the monsoon is far away,
yesterday, a neighbour's child

swore he saw a long black snake
in the park behind our flats.

Catching Up in Strange Times

When I called this morning,
my father told me that just before
going to bed, he'd replaced

the cell in an old alarm clock
because he noticed it had stopped
at 4 p.m. sharp. He didn't have

the strength to set it right,
but all night long he said
he heard it spinning,

and in the morning
when he woke, it had just
about caught up. *I don't*

know what it means, he said,
but these are such strange times,
I knew you would understand.

What Matters

As June slips towards July,
>   the heat turns heavy and wet,

our coolers don't work like they used to,
>   we pray for the rains to return.

We read of atrocities daily;
>   no one is watching the watchmen—

we post angry memes, but we know
>   we're weak when we're inside and distant.

Let's walk through the dark streets, tonight—
>   let's remember what matters, what's true;

the rains will be back soon enough, my friends,
>   soon enough, we'll be back too.

So Long

I want to sing you a sweet song, tonight—
the road you've chosen looks so long, tonight.

When you were small, your dreams were full of dread;
alone, avoiding sleep, you clung to night.

Now fear and walls, and worse, are everywhere:
new plagues, and old, see how they throng our nights?

I know that you can see my shaking hands,
but we'll pretend that I am strong tonight.

The ones you leave will stay to pray and fight;
we'll breathe the scent of rain and dung tonight.

I am your confidante, why doubt me now?
This tide will turn; the moon's still young tonight.

Varavara Rao Came to Delhi Last Night

I was thinking of your poem
'When Moonlight Moves Into the Dark'
as a comrade and I walked past the remnants
of one of Delhi's once wild forests.
From our left came the sound
of rain-soaked branches and wind,
from our right, the grumble and pop
of late-night traffic. Across the road,
beyond the rush of bikes and cars,
loomed the homes of the city's rich—
and I asked myself,
Who owns this hauled-out wealth?
At that moment, I heard you whisper:
All the riches hidden behind closed doors
are the forest.

They want you dead, Varavara Rao,
they think they can silence and cage you,
but we know that is not how this will end.
Not soon, but soon enough, we'll rouse
ourselves from this nightmare to find
vines entwined everywhere,
flames blossoming new worlds.

Note: Italicised lines by Varavara Rao from the poem cited, translated by D. Venkat Rao

Welcoming the Storm

Remember how we threw open the windows
to watch the storm pass over the city—

it arrived just past midnight,
and even after it was so far gone

that we could no longer
hear its thunder,

it still lit up the southern sky
like fireworks at a farmhouse wedding,

or a faulty street light, flickering
over a dark, narrow lane in Mehrauli.

You told me that if I climbed the wobbly,
wooden ladder to the roof,

on a clear day I could see Qutub Minar.
I wasn't sure I believed you,

but I knew you were right to fear the storm
and also to welcome it.

First, We Will Dream It

The late July damp has settled on the city
like a sweat-soaked shirt, but you continue
on the footpath outside the hospital

where workers go to smoke and crows
gather to feed on stale roti and seed.
Further on, across the road,

you give a wide berth to the stinking canine
carcass sprawled in the shade of the shrubs
outside the park's back gate; further still,

you pass the new camp of tarp and twine
that's sprung up in front of the fenced-in ruins
west of the fouled drain's rush.

You're tiring now, but you understand
that if you keep to this path long enough,
you may find a forest and a quiet place to pray.

Late in the night, sweet water will run
through your dreams; you will hear children
splashing somewhere outside your window,

and from the foot of your bed will come
the yelps and gentle whimpers
of a well-fed, sleeping dog.

Last Week, in Hauz Rani Forest
—*for Hany Babu and Varavara Rao*

We met near the pond,
I brought something to eat:

tomatoes, bread,
your favourite sweets—

old couples strolling,
children laughing;

it would have been perfect,
except for these things:

the ducks were caged,
the pond was dry,

there was no breeze,
and I wondered why

we jail our best teachers
and poets.

Only Together Can We Bring It
—*one year after the abrogation*

A year ago, a plague was delivered
upon a far-off northern region,

and many of us in the capital
understood this, but did nothing—

because we were afraid
and felt powerless,

or because we told ourselves
that Twitter or the courts would cure it.

Last night, I watched a storm
flash in the southwest sky—

the ebb and glow of distant light,
just the hint of a cool, clean breeze—

and I wished and prayed
it would bring us relief

from all of this season's
sickness and heat.

Pinjra Tod
—*Delhi, 13 August 2020*

Rain drenched the city
like a bite of ripe pear

after a hot, oily meal,
and there was no dry path

through the narrow lane
behind the masjid,

so two giggling girls
picked their way

through the muddy
maidan—

shoulder-to-shoulder
under one worn umbrella—

while Devangana Kalita
and Natasha Narwal

spent one more long day
in Tihar jail.

With All Due Respect to the Court
—Delhi, 15 August 2020

I tried to type a list of those
imprisoned for 'incitement'—

instead of reading like a poem,
it read like an indictment.

आवारा है

Maybe you'd had too much to drink,
    or maybe you were just dreaming—

or maybe *you* were an *I* or *we*,
    or maybe it does not matter—

but a pack of boys on bikes flew up
    and over the wide, wet crossing,

and six hungry dogs in the market stared
    as we shared a plate of samosas.

Is it right to eat outside, you asked,
    while so many go without?

Nearby, a gang of students sat
    and laughed and flirted and smoked.

It may have been a fever dream,
    or the snack we'd eaten too quickly—

or just the feel of road under feet,
    or maybe it does not matter—

an ancient road roller rumbled by
    as we passed the shuttered temple:

you matched its speed; I slowed and searched
    for demons in puffs of black vapour.

At the T-point by the rubbish heap,
    dogs studied the moon and trembled

as it emerged from a bank of clouds,
    then hung there, like a cradle.

LIFTED AND CARRIED

September—November 2020

Lifted and Carried
—*for Varavara Rao*

It's not hard to remember
    the slow shuffle back,

the way the ceiling fan's
    easy turn makes the hair

on your arms stand up,
    how the morning light

falls with such gentleness
    on every green, growing thing—

how *relief*
    is a seasonal kind of *pleasure*.

We're so quick to forget
    what came before—

the aches, the chills,
    the stabbing, grinding,

burning, heaving, raking,
    cramping, throbbing,

gnawing, shooting—
    perhaps there's just no

advantage in recalling
    such things, but

even after the pain's been replaced
    by your *story* of the pain,

if you are honest, you know
    there were moments

when you thought or wished
    you might shatter or stop,

but also moments when you
    were lifted and carried

by a glass of cool water,
    from a sibling or mother,

a touch on your neck,
    by a comrade or lover,

a quiet, kind word
    from a neighbour or father—

and if you allow yourself
    to examine *these* memories

you will see why
    it's such a heinous crime

to jail innocent people
    for political gain.

I Think of Umar Khalid

When I hear the gentle cooing
of pigeons outside my window,
I think of Umar Khalid,

and when I see crows massing
against an approaching bird of prey,
I think of Umar Khalid.

I think of Umar Khalid
when I see an autowala shaking
his head as he reads the morning news

and when word comes that farmers
and workers are marching again
after so many months of silence.

Just before dawn in Lutyens' Delhi,
the Home Minister wakes with a start—
has he finally gone too far?

Breaking
—Jantar Mantar, 2 October 2020

Last week, we dreamed a feathered thing
dangled high, in tangled wires—

the scent of wood and petrol smoke,
the violent glow of pre-dawn fires;

some terrors are too large to name—
some wounds so deep, they'll never mend—

still, something's breaking in the east;
friends, even this long night will end.

I Fall Asleep Reading a Poem by Akhil Katyal
—*for Natasha Narwal*

I don't smoke, but somehow I'm smoking
on a cramped South Delhi terrace;
I'm looking down at a wide, brown field
of dry grass and scattered trash.
Beyond are trees and more trees,
and gathered in upper branches,
a murder of angry crows
is scolding a circling kite.
Beyond that are just skyscrapers—
or maybe that's just an illusion,
and there is Natasha Narwal,
sipping tea at a roadside dhaba.
I want to go down and ask her
about the food in Tihar Jail,
I want to go down and tell her
how much we all have missed her.

Let Us All Rest in the Company of Those Who Love Us
—*for Varavara Rao*

It settled on me just before dawn
the day after I came to pay my respects—
heavy, like a thick wool blanket
on a not-quite cold night.
It stayed until the scratch
of a distant grass broom
swept it from the room,
like a gentle cloud of dust.

I did not really know him,
so I had no right to grieve,
but I knew what he meant to you,
and when I saw him lying there
in the company of those who loved him,
I remembered an afternoon long ago
when I found my own grandfather
lying still in his bed,
and how my aunt and I sat with him—
and I was so sure I could see
him breathing, but it was only me
that was shaking.

This is not a poem about bail pleas
    or fascism.
Every word I write is against fascism.

Worried Blues Pantoum
—*Delhi, November 2020*

Would you still love me, my friends,
if I lost my sense of smell?
Could we still touch from a distance?
What if I had a dry cough?

If I lost my sense of smell,
would I still crave idli-sambar?
What if I get a dry cough?
I don't go outside; I'm afraid.

Would I still crave idli-sambar?
Would they put a big sign on my door?
I don't go outside, I'm afraid
I might spread this virus to others.

Would they put a big sign on my door?
Would they jail me like Hany Babu?
Could I spread this virus to others
like they spread hatred and lies?

If they jailed me like Hany Babu,
could we still touch from a distance?
In spite of their hatred and lies,
would you still love me, my friends?

Perhaps It's Best
—*nine months after the Delhi Riots*

In spite of the November cold,
    a cat went into heat

and wailed into the night,
    like a sick child

or a faraway ambulance.
    I thought of you then,

and the stray you used to feed;
    I haven't seen her in months.

Perhaps it's best you've gone;
    you told me once how much

you miss the city's sound and light,
    and yes, drying clothes still hang

like strange bursts of bright fruit
    on the rusty barricades

that divide the loud road
    in front of our flat—

but even the healthy among us
    are coughing these days,

and if they don't like how you think,
    they'll come lock you away.

NIGHTFALL AT SINGHU BORDER

November 2020–February 2021

Three Haiku
—*for farmers*

Yesterday morning,
it still seemed impossible:
broken barricades.

The HM paces,
his boss sits in a corner,
growing his white beard.

Nothing stops the tide,
or at dawn, the rising sun—
praise those who feed us.

Nightfall at Singhu Border

By the time you made it past
all the checkpoints and texted,

it was already dark. A line
of tractors, trucks and tents

stretched down the highway
for miles,

and a soft-spoken man
kept trying to explain,

We are not terrorists,
we are here and will stay

so our families and friends
can live decent lives.

The photos you sent on Signal
disappeared before I slept,

but I saw the red flags,
and circles of men sipping tea;

because it was cold,
there were many fires—

as I dreamt,
the fires grew brighter.

Simple Definitions
—*for Kunal Kamra*

When children use kind words,
    it's called a conversation;
and when they argue loudly,
    that's an altercation.

While bullies anywhere
    employ intimidation,
the clever must rely
    on wit and erudition.

When a friend helps calm things down,
    we call that mediation;
in the end, so much depends
    on good communication.

Still, when children can't agree,
    we don't talk of prosecution;
what argument gets solved
    by incarceration?

Some elders have forgotten
    complaints are not sedition,
and tolerance and humour
    are good for the whole nation.

I'll spell it out in case
    you lack imagination:
democracy depends
    on *freedom of expression*

Love Jihad
—*on the first anniversary of the CAA*

Yesterday evening,
as we walked through Kotla Gaon,
the clamour of a ragged wedding band
mingled with the call to prayer,
and for a moment, I swear,
two bright sparks lit up the smoky sky,
and I thought of how worried I'd been
that day last December
when you texted from a police bus
on the outskirts of the city,
and how I bit down on my tongue
when you said that when they freed you,
you would go right back again.
But when we met at Jantar Mantar,
I knew you had been right:

love is always a struggle—
we struggle because we love.

This Number Does Not Exist
—*for Manglesh Dabral*

We were on the run,
and things were changing fast;

one moment, we were huddled
on a windswept rocky ridge in Garhwal

peering down at an approaching line
of police and pack mules,

and the next, we were avoiding
the CCTV cameras

at Haridwar Junction;
you warned me:

Our enemy has many phone numbers,
and I didn't understand you,

but also I did. We finally boarded
a train destined

for the Singhu Border,
or Shaheen Bagh, or home;

when you disappeared, I took
out my phone and dialled you;

a stranger's voice answered,
This number does not exist.

Squatting and shaking
in the space between coaches,

I wrote my father a postcard.
I told him how much I loved him,

and that I was trying to find
my way back.

13 Ways of Looking at a Farmer

The dirt that clings
to the potatoes you hold
came from a farmer's field.

I dreamt a soft-spoken farmer
taught me how to tell
when the corn is ripe.

It was still dark that morning
we heard your uncle
shuffle out to milk the cows;
eighty years old,
and still a farmer.

On the coldest day of December,
a boy grafts a rose onto
a branch of China Orange.
He wants to be a farmer.

Somewhere, the winter
wheat is in the ground;
a farmer looks out
at her field and smiles.

A farmer can tell you
how deep you must drill.

Listen to the creak and splash
of the farmer's hand pump;
tonight there will be a wedding.

On Human Rights Day,
posters of political prisoners
spring up on Tikri border.
Farmers are also humans.

It is cold on the Singhu border;
farmers light fires and plan.

Libraries sprout like tulips;
farmers are readers,
spring has come early.

rupi kaur is writing about farmers—
she just called the PM a tyrant.

Are there three lakh or ten?
Perhaps it does not matter.
Our leaders fear our farmers.

He worked with his hands in the city,
and stood for justice each day;
as he passes, we sing for this farmer—
we grow from seeds he has planted.

Unshakeable
—*Christmas Eve, 2020*

Tonight in Taloja Central Jail,
Father Stan Swamy shakes
but also rejoices;

he knows that soon enough
carpenters, fishers
and blunt-speaking women

will join others who labour—
in fields and factories,
forests and homes—

and that all those who hunger
will be satisfied,

and our weeping
will turn to laughter.

Kiss

Many years ago,
under the influence
of something weaker
than witchcraft
but stronger than black tea,
I kissed a man with a beard.
Our fathers worshipped
different gods, but there
was no mob that night,
no police, no FIR—
just wind and the taste
of sand and damp salt.
I said, friend, I love you so much,
and that is where we left it.

The Moon the MHA and Agent Orange
—*a letter to W.S. Merwin*

Today I am reading *The Moon Before Morning*
I should have read it years ago when a friend
gave it to me but I was lazy and anxious
it is filled with unpunctuated invitations to pause
and shadows and sounds made by rain
right now outside my window I hear the scratch
of a stick broom and the shrill whine of a distant siren
late last night clouds hid the moon and later it rained
and this morning when I took in the newspaper
I saw I had slept through it but I remembered
that I'd woken at dawn to warmth and the gentle
rustle of pigeon wings and that I'd thought
This moment is complete just as it is
yes sometimes I do remember the scent of pine
trees and water and the feel of my grandmother's
hand in my hair and I wish I could return to her
and to that place and to that time when I worried less
yes I am reading your poems with close attention
and I am glad you have found old trees and a quiet garden
near a pond that greets the returning geese each year
but outside my window a sickness has spread
from the Ministry of Home Affairs to Northeast Delhi
and to the forests of Jharkhand and to every place
where people gather around TVs radios and smartphones

and no vaccine cooled by dry ice can stop it
I can see from the final poems in this book that you would
understand what I am saying and also that you would remember
what you wrote five decades ago about the Vietnam War

When the forests have been destroyed their darkness remains

Note: *The last line quoted here comes from an old Merwin poem, 'The Asians Dying'.*

My Mother Calls With Her Worries

Smog has wrapped the city
like a fine wool shawl
when my mother calls to say
she hasn't slept in days—
because of the news on TV
and our friend who is dying.
I know she is right;
these are terrible times,
and we have both always
struggled to calm
the warm flutter in the gut,
the sudden searing
behind the left eye.
I tell her I love her and not to worry:
Delhi's roads are wide enough
for farmers and tractors
and all kinds of lovers—
we'll plough under the wasteland,
plant wheat and white clover.

You'll Join Us, I Know, My Friend
—*for Umar Khalid*

It was late in a South Delhi warehouse,
it was cold, but I didn't feel cold;

Umar Khalid was swaying
to jazz, or was it hip hop?

I looked over his shoulder to see
the Ska Vengers laying it down,

I said, Sir, we're so glad you're here,
how did I miss the news?

He said, don't call me Sir, I'm your friend,
yes, this beats Tihar Jail—

He said, soon we'll be back in the streets;
we're winning, we have to win.

Like That Cat, or Our Constitution
—*Republic Day, 2021*

Sometimes precious things
disappear in a moment,
like the flash and bang
of a wedding cracker
or that cat you used to feed,
caught under a swerving bus;
but sometimes they slip away slowly,
like an early morning dream
where you know you left something
of great value in the train car
you see sinking in the river—
a box of old family photos
perhaps, or the lipstick you took
from your grandmother's table
on the day she died—
and you're glad you're safe on the shore,
but by the time you come fully awake
you cannot remember

where the train was going,
what broke the bridge,
or how many fellow travellers
now lie beneath rushing waters.

A Question for the Court
—*for Munawar Faruqui*

I confess my ignorance
of law and legal matters,

but can you call it *harmony*
when you've outlawed laughter?

Ghazal for a Capital in Darkness

It does not freeze, but nights are cold in the capital;
brave farmers camp on the threshold of the capital.

Farm bills are passed by a voice vote, without counting;
surprising things are bought and sold in the capital.

Ministers pace and kick at walls; they remember:
we don't always do as we are told in the capital.

The British jailed us when we spoke about freedom;
our rulers now are just as bold, in the capital.

These days, they lock students inside Tihar Jail;
dissent and thought are still controlled in the capital.

Last night, goons failed once more to clear protest sites—
the farmers' strength is unequalled in the capital.

Why would a no-name poet sing of this darkness?
There's so much here to love, behold: it's *our* capital!

Postcard from 2019

What if they jailed the students
    and scholars who disagreed

or outlawed peaceful gatherings
    all over the city?

What if they stopped counting
    the votes in parliament

or made it criminal to laugh
    at a court judgement?

If all this came to pass,
    who'd dare speak its name?

And would we even notice if
    other small things changed:

power cuts at the local mosque,
    five times every day,

the space on our front steps where once
    the morning paper lay?

BEHIND THE MASK

February–April 2021

Change

To celebrate, on the day
Munawar Faruqui
was granted bail,
I went to buy a kg
of guavas and oranges.
The fruit seller asked
if he could make change
with one perfect banana
and two handfuls of grapes.
I said, yes, friend,
now why didn't I think of that?

Ten Letters

Somebody planted ten letters, it seems,
on Rona Wilson's computer,

and then police came and took him away,
and later they took many others.

We don't know who planted the letters, my friends,
but they raise an important question:

will anyone dare to investigate
those who led the investigation?

Behind the Mask

some things diminish:
the scent of morning dew
rising off sparse grass;
news of frying food
or what the cat
killed three days back.
After sundown, in crowded
market lanes, we still hear
the clamour of hawkers,
horns, engines, bells,
but we may miss the shift
in the air as we move
from smouldering coals
towards crackling wood—
or the difference between
distant rain and the leaking main
under the road behind the park.
Most nights, my dreams still smell
like worried sweat and roses—

but last night I was locked
in the Home Ministry
it smelled of moth balls mixed
with anger, fear and whisky.

Note to a Fellow Poet on Subtlety and Silence
—*for Nodeep Kaur and Disha Ravi*

You complain I'm too direct,
that similes and slanted images
can unfold truth more powerfully
than the plain truth told plainly,
and that there is wonder afoot
even in this time of darkness
and disease,

but when police and paramilitary forces
lob tear gas at farmers,
it does not cover them like a winter fog,
it covers them like tear gas,
and when they jail young women
for loudly demanding their wages
or for quietly explaining
how to speak loudly,
they are not fencing in spring flowers,
they are jailing young women
who speak up bluntly.

I am trying, my friend, to find
subtle ways to sing in the dark.
But remember, if it ever
comes back to this:

when blood runs in fields or streets
it does not run like warm rain
or a monsoon-fed drain,
it runs like blood,
and when that happens,
subtlety is just silence.

A Simple Prayer
—*after Kabir*

No matter how often you sweep,
dust gathers under your bed
and the TV is loud and shrill;
it sounds like thunder and rust—

but outside, across the main road,
someone has hung out bright clothes
and the tree on the left's raining birdsong;
from its roots rises the scent of spring flowers.

They're sowing division and fear
to silence our songs and our prayers;
but we're only here for a moment—
let's sing of bright cloth and love.

Stopping by Saidulajaib to Consider Horses and Torture
—*for Shiv Kumar*

Hauling carts and vendors home,
weary horses stop to drink
from a bucket on the road
at the edge of Saidulajaib.

They have no time to frisk or roam,
just to quench and shake and blink,
as they pull their heavy loads
up the road by Saidulajaib.

What happens next, I do not know,
except to say their clop and clink
grows softer, softer, as they go
southward from Saidulajaib.

There's news of torture on my phone;
some folks are treated worse, I think,
than the beasts that pull and slow
at the edge of Saidulajaib.

Three Postcards to Umar Khalid

(i)

You don't know me,
but in the summer of 2019,
you met my friend—
she couldn't stop talking about you:
a man who knew how to *listen*,
a leader who spent more time working
out of the spotlight than *in* it;
a scholar who'd learned the art
of switching autos mid-journey—
They trail me everywhere,
you told her, smiling,
Why should I bring them to you?
I was envious I hadn't been there:
for months, I kept hearing your name
spoken alongside words like *hero* and *hope*.
When they put you inside, those words
were joined by rougher ones,
but don't worry;
we have not forgotten.

(ii)

I thought of you last morning
as I passed by the PM's residence
on the way to CP. The wind was cool
and smelled like a green living thing;
the Delhi sky was more blue than grey,

and clouds of bright yellow leaves
rose from a sweeper's broom.
I thought: it's springtime today,
but how long will it last?
My phone said Tihar Jail
was just 12 kilometres away;
at that moment I prayed
that you were near
an open window.

(iii)

Alone at night, or on Delhi's borders
we say your name when we pray or shout;
we have not forgotten you or the others,
we'll welcome you all, when you come out.

I wish we could talk, under a tree,
I'd ask what you'd read, how did you cope?
I'd buy you a cup of special hot tea,
I'd ask what you think of heroes and hope.

Still Trying

I've tried for years to write a perfect poem,
an open window that lets in cool air—

or a siren calling from the main road,
reminding us to listen, reach and care.

That might have worked before this darkness fell,
but now, I fear, it may not be enough;

we must throw back the curtains so the bright sky
can cleanse this sickness, feed our strength and love.

Coronation

We stood in the shadows and ate,
it looked like a coronation;
how we got in, I'm not sure,
perhaps we snuck in the back.
It could have been Jaipur or London,
or maybe the Central Vista—
the music was loud and fast,
and most of the crowd was dancing.
You said you heard screams from below,
but nobody seemed to notice—
you looked like you might pass out;
I felt the room start to spin.
A painting that hung by the throne
showed fires and families fleeing;
another showed farmland circled
with walls of concrete and wire.
A man in a suit whispered, smiling:
We've finally figured it out—
business is booming, my friend,
the good times are here at last.

News of Sickness and Health

Umar Khalid smiles and raises his fist
on his way out of court

and an 83-year-old priest is denied bail
in the '*collective interest of the community*'.

Meanwhile in Myanmar,
protesters disappear in the night

and a striking worker
tells a reporter,

'*They are the king now,
but we are not their servants.*'

Questions I Don't Need to Ask

Do you struggle against
the deepening dark
because you read
Marx or Ambedkar?
Or was it the bus driver
who whispered in your ear,
or the teacher who failed you,
or the neighbours who
forced you to say,
'Everything is fine'?

Or was it the way
the world treated your parents—
or was it the way
they still loved you?

Abolish Our Local Police
—*for Natasha Narwal and Devangana Kalita*

Maybe it's just habit,
but even all these months after
they locked down the city
and took away friends of your friends,
sometimes you still float away
at that moment when light's fading
and the first bats are flying;
and when you wake with a start
it is already dark—
you're not sure where you are,
but you hear the door bang—
and then you're relieved
to find it's a friend
who wants to play cards—
or the newspaper man,
bringing the bill—
not someone who's come
to take you away:

*we don't need the police,
they only spread fear.*

Reel for Delhi in Springtime

When I tell you what it means
to me to live in Delhi,

I won't use trending music
or a dozen flashing photos

approved by the Ministry
of Tourism—

just a few *words*
to conjure images—

that pair of young women
brushing shoulders

as they sip tea on the edge
of the dusty maidan—

or the thin, strong man
in the next lane over

who right now
is stripping off his shirt

as he assesses a growing
pool of stinking water—

and on a good day,
this might be enough

to get you to consider
this simple idea:

we can remake this world;
we can, and we must, my friends.

LATE APRIL PRAYER FOR DELHI

April–June 2021

Failure in Gujarat

When I saw the video of pyres
burning in an open field
because, contrary to what one
would expect based on official figures,
the crematoriums were overflowing,
I remembered that spring day,
two years ago,
when I saw you last,
and how your mother's
shoulders slumped
as the steel doors slammed,
and how late that night,
after the tears and prayers
and stories boiled down,
we sat in silence
under a spinning fan,
and then how she looked
at me and said,

I know you know I loved her—
but still, I feel I have failed.

A Late April Prayer for Delhi

The moon is nearly full,
the pyres are burning bright;

the wind is clear and cool—
let the air last through this night.

I Have Seen Astonishing Sights
—*after Kabir*

Friends, I have seen
astonishing sights:
a great seer slain
by invisible invaders;

proud men queuing
for buses, or liquor,
to flee a failing capital;
kings and princes
kissing their master's
hidden hand
while their subjects
struggle to breathe—
I have seen
the fevered rich
party, then pack
their bags
while pyres burn
day and night.

I saw one woman
turn her scooty
into an ambulance,
and just now I saw
another woman

sitting on the footpath
in front of a hospital—
she is less than a mile
from where I stay;
she is sobbing,
my friends,
she is sobbing.

In Front of the Chemist

one man cuts the distanced queue
to buy a tube of toothpaste;
we shake our heads,

but in this heat,
who has the strength
to shout?

Some time later,
another man approaches,
and says in a shaking voice:

*Please, I need two face
shields, please—
I must go to the hospital now.*

We shuffle our feet and bow
our heads; for once,
we're all glad to give way.

For a Tender Comrade
—*Delhi, 1 May 2021*

This morning, you said you'd dreamt
of a room full of books and children;

I only remember warm air,
the sound of your breath and sirens.

Delhi Emergency, 10 p.m.

Outside the emergency
department doors,
a woman sobs
as she clings
to a trembling,
straight-backed man.
As we pass them,
everything shakes:
the smoky clouds,
the hospital walls—
bushes, flowers, trees—
the footpath
under our feet.
These two are holding up
a piece of the sky tonight;
       it has broken,
             I know
  you can feel it.

Divinations

I dreamed of hillsides littered
with bundles of burning wood:

death is all around us;
there is no other way to read this.

I woke to news of more bodies
gathering in the Ganga:

it was a kind of protest;
there is no other way to read this.

News in Review
—*Delhi, 15 May*

१.

Our PM works hard
on his palace and speeches;
'Let's be positive.'

Vaccine centre's closed;
an old woman asks, 'How long?'
'Try again at dawn.'

२.

The HM's police
have withdrawn from Delhi's streets;
still the sirens wail.

They locked up our friends
but did not send oxygen:
we will not forget.

३.

Far from the city,
neighbours die of breathlessness;
something is not right.

Bodies float downstream:
this is not a metaphor,
just friends we couldn't save.

For My Mother, That Baby and Father Stan Swamy

The day my mother calls
to confess she'd woken in tears
(she still misses *her* mother,
after so many years),
I am blessed to meet
a six-week-old baby girl;
drunk on her mother's milk,
she smiles as she sleeps
sprawled on a charpai,
like a pehlwan
after a hard-won match.
Later that night,
I read that Stan Swamy
can no longer walk or bathe
or even feed himself,
and how he's told the court
he does not prefer a hospital
to Taloja Jail; he prefers
to suffer and die in prison—
or to go *home*:
'Whatever happens to me,
I'd like to be with my own.'

HOW IS IT WE KEEP FORGETTING

August 2021—June 2022

Failed Ghazal
—*15 August 2021*

I spent hours last night
trying to write a ghazal

that included this line:
unbroken, Umar Khalid's still in jail,

and also this one:
they aim to break your soul and will in jail.

'School teachers' and 'freedom fighters'
figured in it,

but I gave up in the end
because it really all came down to this:

They aim to break your soul and will in jail;
unbroken, Umar Khalid's still in jail.

Song for You
—Jasola Vihar, 6.24 p.m.

Let's walk out into the light, my love!
Why not? There's time before night, my love.

This sky is hard to define, it's true;
both bats and birds are in flight, my love.

Recall how we shivered for hours that night—
Shaheen Bagh was crowded and bright, my love.

This morning, rain washed our smoky sky;
Hany Babu's still jailed tonight, my love.

A coward, yes; I've surrendered my name—
to this broken world, I write my love.

Elegy for Lakhimpur Kheri

The marching farmers fall,
like wheat beneath a fast combine;

young and old, they fall,
struck from behind, struck from behind!

Watch the video:
it is so clear, my friends, so clear;

they're marching peacefully:
they do not fear, they do not fear.

I see my father there;
his tall, bent back, his slow, slow gait.

The fallen ones will rise—
like seeds, that is their fate, our fate!

Facing the NIA
—*Dyal Singh College Road, 9 p.m.*

Emerging from the metro,
I met a swollen moon,

I sipped a little smoke,
tripped on the NIA.

There was Hany Babu
singing out a lecture—

it was so soft and clear;
it sounded like a poem.

I sat down on the footpath,
I shivered, yes, I cried:

how can we celebrate
with friends like this inside?

Dreams of Fear and Rejoicing

Last week I crossed a narrow bridge
strung over a wide canyon,

and as I crossed, I felt a hole
open in my belly.

Last night under a swollen moon,
I dreamt of Umar Khalid;

I heard him laughing in his cell:
The farmers have prevailed!

What They're Selling

These days on the metro,
I keep seeing this pair:

the old guy with his thick
white beard,

and his orange-robed friend—
the one who's always smiling.

They're building homes
and universities;

handing out jobs
and free vaccines.

I feel dizzy sometimes,
thinking about the possibilities:

a superhighway to Lanka;
my very own flying chariot.

A Memory, a Prayer and a Dream
—*Christmas Day, 2021*

i.

One morning, during the plague
that followed the fires
that scarred the capital,

you were feeding our pet rat,
when word came
from the town cryer:

The farmers have circled the city.

ii.

Several years and many deaths later,
the king and his first minister
finally concede.

It will take another long year
to pry open the jails,
but when spring arrives that March,

Shaheen Bagh is back in bloom.

iii.

'The change' comes fast when it comes:
the police and army trade their lathis
and guns for the tools they need

to build homes and hospitals.
On every corner, libraries sprout,
like winter wheat planted

over obsolete borders.

Sheep
—1 January 2022

Flocks of sheep
drift down from the hills,

like dry leaves blown free
by a gust of winter wind—

they block highways,
refuse any compromise.

In Lutyens' Delhi, the Home
Minister paces and shouts:

Who's in charge of the sheep?
I told you to crush all resistance!

The Censor at Work in the Park

You said you'd been
weighing the cost

of self-censorship
and looked pained

when I let slip
a laugh.

Forgive me, my friend,
I could not explain:

it was not about you,
but what I cannot say.

'If They Are So mighty, Let Them Snuff Out the Moon'
—*writing from Tihar Jail,*
Umar Khalid quotes Faiz Ahmad Faiz

In the photos the young lovers post,
they are smiling as they sip
from the same bottle of cola,
they are sharing a plate of chaat,
they are sitting on a seesaw,
under the bright,
winter moon.
Some nights he says,
I'm cold, please warm
my hands. Some nights
she says, *Let us pray*
now for Umar Khalid;
I hear he is lonely inside.

Delhi Weekend Curfew
—*January 2022*

The dull, orange moon
was hanging there,
a dusty, swollen ache.

The guard said, *Close
your phone*—you said,
friend, it's just the moon.

He shrugged his shoulders
and looked down—
what was left to say?

This waning moon,
this smoky sky—
the orders we all take.

I Fall Asleep Reading Uday Prakash as Russia Invades Ukraine

I'm dressed in my best
at the wedding hall,
or is it a gym in Saket?

I'm not ready to marry
but don't want to fight,
so I slip out for a smoke.

I meet a sweeper,
we chat for a moment,
he shows me a hollow wall—

there's cash behind it,
he says, please take some—
it's black, but free, for now.

Later, I'm sipping
tea at a dhaba
somewhere in Dhaula Kuan;

a plateless car
pulls up, and then
a tinted window rolls down:

The HM and Putin
laugh as they ask
for samosas and directions;

Ayodhya's their goal,
there's not much time,
the fifth phase is nearly here.

> *(Just before dawn, the northern sky
> fills with neon lightning—*
>
> *thunder follows fast behind:
> the sound of young men dying.)*

Closer, Closer

Armed men lining city streets,
reporters sent to jail;

intestines spilt in sand or snow,
apartment buildings, rubble.

Last night I dreamt of fire and bombs,
I woke at dawn, trembling—

I asked you for the news from home—
you said Kashmir is angry.

How Is It We Keep Forgetting?
—*While reading Ilya Kaminsky,*
 I Think of Umar Khalid

Just outside Qutub Minar
there's a line of buses and cars

filled with all kinds of folks,
looking for all kinds of things—

some have come to lose themselves;
some just want to get home;

walking back to the metro,
we pass flocks of uneasy dogs.

Later, I read *Deaf Republic*,
under a whirling fan—

Delhi is not a mythical town,
but they've jailed the best among us.

A War Poem

Once while going by sleeper
from Delhi to Bengaluru

I dreamt I was trapped
in a broken mine shaft,

and waking, I cried
out in terror.

Now I dream of distant fires
and wonder how far they will spread—

there's no way to know,
but this much is plain:

there's no glory in war,
just sorrow and pain,

there's no glory in war—
all war is the same.

No Escape

Last night, I tried to turn
off words and worries,
to let the city rush over me,

like a postmodern raag,
written for engine, horn,
shout and bark—

after the elections in UP,
I stopped reading the news,
but the pigeons outside

my window keep cooing:
Madhya Pradesh,
Jahangirpuri—

and the raucous crows
won't stop their calls:
Bulldozers, bulldozers—

they'll be here soon!
Bulldozers, bulldozers,
what will you do?

Ghazal Against Bulldozers

Who authorises homes and rites in this city?
Each one who lives here has a right to this city!

Equality under the law is just fiction—
bulldozers show their masters' might in this city.

Landlords and agents act like sponges and thugs—
private property? A blight on this city.

The cops say, 'with you, for you, always'—but we know:
they'll come for us, morning or night, in this city.

Who reads alone in Tihar Jail? Umar Khalid!
Behind the smoke, the moon is bright in this city.

You ask me what it cost to give up my name—
Nothing, and now I'm free to write in this city.

Father Stan Swamy Came to Delhi Last Week

I was sitting near the back
at the launch of G.N. Saibaba's
book of poems and letters from prison
when he slipped into the seat on my left—
I might not have noticed,
but his white hair was glowing
like a Christmas star,
or a tube light hung on the wall
behind the priest at Midnight Mass.
His tremors were mostly gone;
I only saw him shake once—
when A.S. Vasantha Kumari
described the solitary confinement
cells in Nagpur Central Jail.
He disappeared before the Q and A,
but later, as I stood outside with friends
giving thanks for the cool May rain,
we heard him whisper as he passed:

Breathe deep, comrades, breathe deep—
tonight you can smell the forest

Acknowledgements

I owe a great debt to Urvashi Bahuguna and A.A.W. for their careful readings and comments on early versions of this manuscript—and to Ajitha G.S. for her help with the final edits. I am thankful for all the help this effort has got from a few unnamed friends, near and far. Thanks also to Saurabh Garge for the cover art; and to V. Shwetha and the whole team at Westland for doing the many needful things that go into making a book. And, of course, to Karthika V.K.–for her ear, and also her courage.

Versions of some of these poems appeared first in *The Penguin Book of Indian Poets*, *Rattle*, *Scroll.in*, *The Alipore Post*, *nether Quarterly*, *The Sunflower Collective*, *India at 75* and *LiveWire*.

www.ingramcontent.com/pod-product-compliance
Lightning Source LLC
LaVergne TN
LVHW010327070526
838199LV00065B/5679